## DE

This book is dedicated to all the hardworking
women that put their heart and soul into car business.
They make this business fun and exciting and I owe
everything I know about the business to the people I
meet in the dealerships on the daily basis.

Special thanks to my wife for the enormous patience it takes to be married to me.  You are the best!

*If you are in it to win it then Max is your guy!  He will help you make money, increase customer retention, and keep you compliant.*

Julio Batista
General Manager
Teddy Nissan and VW

## DO NOT SKIP THIS SECTION

I LOVE CAR BUSINESS!  Everything I have I owe to car business.  It made me the person I am today; throughout the years I've met great people that I am proud to call friends and colleagues.

But what I see in the industry is pretty alarming and making me scratch my head.  Automotive retail is at crossroads—either we get better or we will be extinct.

So I decided to write a book and make a bunch of videos about #CrazyShitCarDealersDo.  This book is not written for the benefit of consumers but for the benefit of dealer principals, general managers, dealership employees as well as all the vendors that service car dealers.

My goal is to shed the light on #CrazyShitCarDealersDo in order to protect the industry from self-destruction.

*Car dealers are not just good at selling cars; they are absolutely amazing at digging their own grave.*

This book is unique because it covers insanity that takes place in all departments of a car dealership. You will recognize a lot of familiar topics affecting Sales, BDC, F&I, HR, Fixed Ops, and general management.

**Think of this book as a sales pitch and what I am selling is pretty simple stuff—KEEP DOING WHAT YOU ARE DOING AND BE OUT OF BUSINESS.**

I am fortunate to grow up in the business and work in every department of a car dealership. I started as sales person and throughout the years worked as a sales manager, finance manager, general sales manager, service manager, and general manager. I ended my automotive retail career running an auto group that broke multiple sales and gross profit records.

I moved on to providing income development services through F&I products and training and later opened Total Dealer Compliance—one of the best dealership compliance firms in the country.
In addition to F&I and Compliance I provide dealership consulting services that are focused on process improvement, customer retention, and profitability.

My experience uniquely qualifies me to write this book because I know the business and see it from several angles.  There is no particular sequence to the book and that is by design.  I want you to keep reading instead of just focusing on one specific topic or department.  This will help you see the big picture.

**I truly hope that this book will be a wake-up call for car dealers across the country.  Please reach out to me and I will help you make the magic happen.  The magic is customer satisfaction that translates into customer retention that in turn translates into more sales and more profits.**

**Max Zanan**
**917-903-0312**
**max@maxzanan.com**

# 1. Not recognizing the threat of digital retail.

Amazon and Uber completely retrained all of us when it comes to convenience and transparency. Here is what I mean: when you buy anything from Amazon you know exactly how much you paid for that item and when it will be delivered to your house. When you order an Uber you know when the car is going to be in front of your house, make and model, name of the driver, rating of the driver, and most importantly how much it is going to cost you to go from point A to point B.

It is logical for consumers to expect this level of transparency and convenience when shopping for a car. Unfortunately most car dealerships are in a position to provide this level of experience yet.

***What is really alarming is that majority of car dealerships do not think that they need to change their sales process.***

A lot of car dealers actually think that customers enjoy spending 6 hours in the showroom trying to buy a car. They are convinced that people love to haggle. Even though there are numerous surveys and studies that say that customers would rather go to a dentist or fly across country in the middle seat before they go to a dealership.

Car dealers are human and humans are afraid of change. The real fear here is that transparency and convenience will negatively impact profits. So here is the question: Do you want to be Barnes & Noble or Amazon, Blockbuster or Netflix?

Don't be afraid of change because if you are someone else will eventually eat your lunch. Not to mention the fact that people are willing to pay premium for convenience and transparency. You don't have to give cars away. Just take a look at the prices Carvana charges; they are not by far the cheapest.

Start incorporating a digital storefront into your website. The sooner you do it the sooner you will find out what is the consumers' appetite for e-commerce in your area and the sooner you will start making changes to your sales process.

Here is a final thought: digital retail means disrupting your business. If you do not do it then someone else will. Just ask Kodak. Kodak invented digital photography but never attempted to introduce it because it would disrupt their (very profitable) analog film business. And now the company is bankrupt.

## 2. Not recognizing the threat of Carvana.

At the time of this writing Carvana's market cap is 4.63 Billion with a B. It is more than 50% higher than Autonation's. Meanwhile Autonation is the largest publicly-held auto group in the country with more than 360 retail outlets. In addition, Autonation is a real auto group because it has new and used car departments as well as parts and service. Carvana, on the other hand, is just a used car dealer. Let that sink in for a moment.

Currently Carvana is in 84 markets, they sold 25,000 last quarter, they are averaging $2300 per car and strongly feel that they will get to $3000 per car in the near future.

Now we all know that it is really hard to make money selling new cars since we live in the environment of compressed margins. Majority of car dealers rely on their used car departments for additional revenue/profits. Every time Carvana sells a car it is chipping away at your used car profit.

Now let's assume for a moment that rolling out in as many markets is just phase one. What if phase two is Carvana service centers. Again car dealers rely on fixed ops revenue/profits to survive and if Carvana is going to chip away at used car and fixed op revenue then you have to ask yourself a question – How is my dealership going to keep the doors open?

So what is the formula of Carvana's success? They come as close to the Amazon experience as humanely possible. ***Complete transparency, home delivery, and 7 day return policy.***

What are you doing to compete with Amazon? I am yet to meet a dealer who embraced complete transparency, home delivery, and a return policy.

Complete transparency, home delivery, and 7 day return policy are the elements of Carvana's success. The real driver behind it is the consumers' dissatisfaction with the sales process in the brick and mortar car dealerships. Car dealers need to fix their processes before it is too late. I am going to end this chapter with a scary thought:

***What are you going to do when Amazon buys Carvana?....***

### 3. No long-term vision.

I am the first to admit that when I was in retail we didn't have a long-term vision. Our time horizon was 30 days. How many cars are we going to sell this month? And on the first of each month I would go from hero to zero. Not much has changed since then. Car dealers are in perpetual rat race and 30 day reporting cycle is destroying the business.

This rat race prevents car dealers from developing a long-term strategy and makes it almost impossible to react to the market changes. Majority of publicly traded companies report on a quarterly basis and even that is often criticized by investors because it places all the focus on the short-term success and that in turn might not align with long-term sustainability of the business.

Here is a perfect example—Barnes & Noble didn't want to develop an e-reader because they felt that there was no market for it and it would negatively impact their profit and loss statement. Meanwhile Amazon grabbed a 90% market share with Kindle and by the time Barnes & Nobel came out with Nook it was too late.

When was the last time you had a meeting with your senior management team to discuss plans for the next 6 months, year, or even 3 years? My guess is – probably never. While you are chasing a number here are few things your dealership most likely missed:

- Change in shopping habits
- Importance of online reviews
- Emergence of Carvana
- Emergence of OEM subscriptions
- And the list goes on....

Jack Welch, former CEO of General Electric says it best:

*"Management is about managing in the short term, while developing the plans for the long term. Any jerk can have short-term earnings. You squeeze, squeeze, squeeze, and the company sinks fiver years later."*

4.  **Not revolting against OEM stair-step programs.**

Carmakers are destroying automotive retail through stair-step programs. Chasing factory money negatively impacts sales process because at some point you start selling the price or the payment NOT the car. In addition, car dealers are willing to take ridiculous deals on the last day of the month if they are short a few units. So now there is customer that gets a deal that you wouldn't give your brother or aunt and this customer is forever retrained to expect this type of a deal in the future.

Let's take a look at the OEM stair-step programs from the perspective of dealership compliance. I am convinced that majority of deceptive advertising is due to these stair-steps programs. In addition, deceptive trade practices taking place in the finance department (falsifying credit apps and jamming F&I products) are also due to desperation of a dealer to hit the "magic" number.

It takes guts to realize that customer experience is much more important than short-term financial gain from below the line factory money. *Customer experience will carry you through the next sales downturn. Never forget that.*

I don't understand why car dealers do not lobby their factories to put an end to the stair-step! It will help improve customer experience and build value in the product.

Not to mention that as a business owner you want to be in control of your destiny instead of blindly chasing an unrealistic number that makes some senior VP in corporate look good.

## 5. Not understanding the value of human resources.

Sales department is the face of your dealership. We can all agree that experienced employees provide better customer service, sell more cars, and represent your company in the best way possible. It is extremely beneficial for any dealership to have a great team *so why is there a 70% turnover in the sales department?*

Let's start with the fact that most car dealerships do not have a dedicated HR manager. Now, during the lowest unemployment in modern history, more than ever car dealers need to attract, develop, and retain talent. If your dealership doesn't approach HR function systematically it will be progressively harder to stay competitive. *Do not forget that at the end of the day people buy from people and you organization must have the best people.*

It is imperative to develop an organizational culture and then immerse new hires in it. Start with creating a mission statement and a list of core organizational values. Follow that with a code of ethics. Display your Code of Ethics in the showroom and on the website. Make sure your employees sign off on it every year during the review process. Ask yourself a simple question—Why would someone want to work in your dealership? Do you offer training, career advancement, reasonable schedule or you are one of the dealers that offers zero training, dead-end job, and bell-to-bell hours?  Do you have an effective onboarding process for new hires or you just say "there is the car, go sell it."

What are you doing to attract talent?  When was the last time your dealership participated in a high school or college job fair?  Have you developed onboarding curriculum?

Talented people will not show up at your door on their own so you must create a full-time HR manager position in order to stay competitive.  Stop wasting money on blow-up gorillas and go after quality people.

***Do not think that sales department turnover is the only issue.  It is extremely difficult to find good mechanics and finance managers.  I promise that your full time HR manager will be very busy....***

## 6.  **Still advertising in print.**

You don't live under a rock, you know newspaper readership is down, you know newspapers are becoming extinct.  So why do you still advertise there?!

You are not naïve, you know that nobody buys a paper because they are looking for a car.  So why do you still advertise there?!

You know there are better ways to allocate your advertising dollars.  There is Facebook, Google, Instagram, LinkedIn, Cars.com, Autotrader, and the list goes on.

Ask yourself a simple question—When was the last time you bought a newspaper because you wanted to buy anything?  The answer is not once in over a decade...

I doubt any car dealer can make a compelling argument why they are still advertising in print.  More importantly I doubt that a newspaper can make a compelling argument why your dealership should advertise with them.

## 7. Being busy doing the same thing.

Jeff Bezos runs Amazon and is the richest man in the world. He gets paid for making critical decisions about strategy and implementation. Decision-making is hard and painful but it separates men from boys.

Majority of car dealers are a different breed. It is as if they are not interested in long-term viability of their business. They also feel that they know it all and therefore need no help.

I am in dealerships every day and sometimes when I walk-in to a new store I feel as if I am being teleported into 1980's. More often than not if I ask to speak to the dealer principal the answer is that he or she is busy. Busy designing a newspaper ad? Busy ordering rust proofing?

Dealer principals you have a responsibility to your family, employees, and customers and you need as much information as possible in order to survive the cataclysmic shifts taking place in automotive retail. Do yourself a favor – take meetings, learn new things, and attend conferences to ensure survival of your business.

*You can't operate as if it is 1985 and expect to survive in 2019.*

## 8. Not spending enough on marketing to existing customers.

Whenever I ask dealer principals and general managers how much they spend per car on advertising most of them have a pretty accurate idea. It usually varies anywhere from $200--$800 per car depending on the franchise, credit profile of a buyer, whether dealer is interested in selling used or new cars, so on and so forth. Basically, they know their new customer acquisition cost.

Whenever I ask them how much they spend marketing to their sold customers I usually get a blank stare. Intuitively we all know that sold customers are our best customers assuming they were treated right. They are the driving force behind word of mouth advertising, referral, and repeat business. *So why do car dealers completely neglect them after the sale?* Why do car dealers set up their CRM to start following up with sold customers 60 days prior to their lease maturity date?

*Wouldn't it be so much cheaper to keep in touch with sold customers and transition them to the service department, collision shop, and then back to sales department? Wouldn't it be so much cheaper to set-up a loyalty program and let customers accumulate points that they can use towards the purchase of the new car or a repair in the service department? Wouldn't be a great idea to reward customers with points for each referral, positive review on social media, or a great survey?*

Why aren't dealers allocating advertising dollars towards marketing their service department in order to increase customer retention?  Car dealers make it way too easy for Jiffy Lube and Firestone to stay in business…

Why are car dealers not getting in touch with sold customers just to say hello, to make sure that everything is OK with the car?  Caring about your customers will ensure that Carvana or any other disrupter cannot threaten your business.

## 9. Not actively promoting service and parts departments.

Here is a simple experiment – Google "oil change near me" or "oil change and the zip code." I guarantee you will see Valvoline, Jiffy Lube, Midas, and Firestone on the first page. Most likely you will not see your car dealership or any other car dealership on the first page of search results. Now Google – "oil filter for Toyota Camry" and I promise you will see listings from Amazon, Autozone, Advanced Auto Parts, and NAPA. Again most likely you will not see your dealership or any other car dealership on the first page of search results. This is all you need to know to conclude that car dealers are completely neglecting their parts and service departments.

Like I said before car dealers make it too easy for independent mechanics and aftermarket parts stores to stay in business. Their entire business models are based on the fact that car dealers cannot retain their own customers.

Car dealers are so focused on selling cars that they ignore the fact that there is a lot of money to be made in parts and service. Not to mention that it is your parts and service departments that will carry you through the next sales downturn. And of course happy service customers are much more likely to buy another car from you.

***So what are you doing to promote your parts and service departments?*** Is search engine optimization and pay-per-click part of the advertising budget? Are you retailing parts online? Are you marketing to Do It Yourself community? Are you giving away dealer-owned pre-paid maintenance or offering Engine for Life program?

Make sure that your Parts & Service Director is present when you work on the advertising budget. Do not take the easy way out and just do an OEM oil change mailer. Get creative!

Or you are just hoping that customers somehow will just show up in your service drive. Remember that hoping is not an effective strategy. Blockbuster was hoping that customers would just show up in their video stores...

## 10.     Selling OEM pre-paid maintenance, vehicle service contracts, and ancillary products.

Let's be honest carmakers can barely build a car that consumers want.  If you think I am being too harsh then please explain Pontiac Aztec or Chevy Cruze or SmartCar.  So what makes you think that OEMs have any expertise when it comes to F&I products?

Take OEM pre-paid maintenance or vehicle service contracts.  If your dealership sells these you are basically encouraging your customers to go elsewhere to do the work.  It is great for OEMs but not so great for your business.  Consider selling or giving away pre-paid maintenance that is only good at your service department.  This way your service retention will go through the roof and your service advisors will be able to build a relationship with customers.  This relationship will come in handy when the time comes to upsell real repair work.

Here is an added bonus—you will keep the forfeiture (premium not used because customers never showed-up) not the OEM.

Also, sell third-party service contracts; better yet sell dealer-branded service contracts because it helps with service retention and F&I profits.  Autonation attributes increase in F&I profits to the sale of Autonation-branded F&I products.

And don't forget that non-OEM products are cheaper. Not too mention that you can reinsure your F&I products and build a nest egg for the expansion or retirement.

## 11. Not having a comprehensive compliance program.

Breaking news—customers don't trust you and law enforcement agencies do not like you.  Here is how it all comes together:

- You are under pressure to sell cars because of the stair-step program
- You engage in deceptive advertising to get customers to come to the showroom
- You put pressure on your F&I department to make something out of nothing because you can't deliver losers that you are advertising
- Your finance department engages in falsification of credit applications, payment packing, and jamming F&I products to make up the losses on the front-end
- Customers come out of the ether and want to cancel products or the entire transaction
- There is no effective complaint resolution process so the customer escalates his or her complaint to Attorney General or Federal Trade Commission
- Number of complaints triggers an investigation that results in hundreds of thousands and sometimes in millions of dollars in fines and penalties
- Consumers' negative view of car dealers is reinforced through headlines in newspapers and TV

- Consumers search for a better way to buy a car; hence Carvana

Comprehensive compliance program can help you improve customer experience and reduce liability associated with fines and penalties.

**So why so many car dealers do not spend a penny on compliance program?**

First, it requires a change in behavior and the fear is that compliance equals reduced gross profit. Second, it means spending money and it is so much better to get a blow-up gorilla. Ultimately it might mean disrupting your own business and who wants to do that?! Let's just wait for Carvana to do it for us...

CONTACT ME TO SET-UP A COMPREHENSIVE COMPLIANCE PROGRAM IN YOUR DEALERSHIP:

917-903-0312
max@maxzanan.com

## 12.    Not using social media.

Whenever I come across a dealership's Facebook page I feel like exactly zero thought went into making it. Posts are boring, there is almost no video, and no customer engagement. You are better off without a Facebook page if this is how you are doing it.

There is also more to social media than a Facebook page. There is Instagram, LinkedIn, YouTube, etc. Effective use of social media will help tell a story about your dealership, your employees, your involvement in the community. Social media is not there to promote a $299 per month lease special. The goal is to make your existing and future customers get to know your organization and for you to make a compelling argument why they should buy from you.

I want to encourage dealer principals and general managers to embrace social media and produce content on a daily basis. It takes hard work, discipline, and getting out of your comfort zone but it is totally worth it.

Your website and social media channels must become a resource to your customers. Post video walkarounds, how to videos (how to use navigation, how to take the top down, how to change oil, etc.), interview with employees, and happy customers. This type of content is much more likely to go viral compared to endless specials.

Remember I mentioned that you need a full-time HR manager. Guess what? You also need a full-time social media manager. Having your 16 year old son or daughter is not going to cut it anymore.

Having interesting content will help you grow your social media following and that in turn will reduce your marketing costs and you will be able to convert a percentage of your followers into buyers.

***Again you have to throw out your old playbook and get with the times.***

## 13.     Not understanding the value of online reviews.

Let's assume for a second that none of your customers would ever file a complaint with Attorney General or Federal Trade Commission.  Instead they would go home and blast your dealership on every social media outlet known to men.

- Google
- Yelp
- Facebook
- Instagram
- LinkedIn
- DealerRater
- Cars.com
- Autotrader.com
- CarGurus.com
- Twitter
- Snapchat

At this point I am not sure what is worse—complaints or bad reviews.  Once your organization accumulates an X amount of bad review it will start negatively impacting your floor traffic and sales.  Customers do not just research the car they want to buy; they also research a dealership where they are going to buy it.  Car buyers are no different than you and I.  Let's say you want to take you husband or wife out for dinner.  You get online to do a quick research and read reviews.  When was the last time you told your spouse "Honey we absolutely must check out this one star Italian restaurant." Car buyers do the same thing; they are willing to travel further as long as they can get a good experience.

The flip side is the good reviews. ***Why aren't you actively soliciting good reviews from your customers?*** Why do I see car dealerships that have been in business for decades with less than 200 reviews?! Why do I see dealerships with 1 star on Yelp or 3.5 stars on Google?! Anything below 4.9 is a failure!

What are you doing to obtain customer reviews? Is there a bonus in place for sales people that get the most customer reviews? Are you using reputation management software that allows you to ask the customer to write one review and distribute it to multiple reviews? Are you responding to negative reviews in a timely manner?

If the answer is No then don't be surprised why the floor traffic is going down, sales are decreasing, and gross profit is evaporating.

## 14.     Not resolving customer complaints effectively.

99.99% of customers will go back to the selling dealer to resolve an issue and if your dealership doesn't have an effective complaint resolution process customers will either escalate their complaints to law enforcement agencies or destroy your dealership's reputation online.  Either way you lose.

First, your compliance officer is the best person to handle customer complaints because his compensation is not based on commission.  It is unrealistic to expect a general manager, sales manager, or a sales person to objectively handle customer complaints.

Second, it is the best practice to have a Customer Complaints or Customer Concerns tab on your dealership website.  This way customers fill out a form and have it routed to your compliance officer for timely resolution.

Now the real question is how do you effectively resolve customers' complaints.  I thought about it long and hard and here is the answer:

***You either give money back or take the car back.***
Sometimes you have to do it even if you didn't do anything wrong because you are better off losing a battle but winning the war.  The war that I am talking about is an investigation by a law enforcement agency or an avalanche of negative reviews.

## 15.     Refusing to service cars that were bought elsewhere.

You've got to be kidding me!  So just because you failed to sell a car you penalize the customer by refusing to service their car?!  I will say it again--you've got to be kidding me!

Let's examine this logic—instead of spending your time and energy on improving the sales process you choose to lose this customer forever.  Instead of enjoying fixed ops revenue that comes from scheduled maintenance, repairs, and recalls you choose to make a point by refusing to service the customer's car.

Don't tell me that your shop capacity is maxed out and you want to do the right thing by the customers that bought cars from you.  **_Have you ever thought of being open an extra shift or 24 hours?_**

Do you honestly think that turning away a customer will make them buy a car from you in the future?  Let me help you out here—the answer is absolutely not and you are only making it easier for your competitors.

## 16.      Not offering 0% APR financing for repairs in service department.

A little over 30% of Americans has enough savings to cover a $1000 emergency. That means that over 60% of Americans couldn't afford to repair their car.

Out of warranty repair work could be very profitable because a vast majority of independent mechanics do not have the necessary training or the necessary special tools to do the work. Don't forget that you make a 50% mark-up on parts and 75% mark-up on labor. If you examine your effective labor rate on complex repairs you would see that it goes up to $300 an hour. Amazon would kill for margins like these.

***So why isn't your service department offering 0% APR financing for repairs over $500?***

It is your responsibility as the business owner to accommodate your customers. Don't make it hard for your customers to work with you. Advertise no interest financing on your website, include it in your other marketing campaigns. Just imagine how much more effective a marketing campaign targeting out-of-warranty vehicles would be if you offered 0% financing.

## 17. Not having regular sales training in service department.

Majority of dealer principals and general managers came up through sales and they have a real appreciation for sales training. That's why Saturday sales training takes place in majority of car dealerships in the country.

Somehow car dealers do not view service advisors as sales people; they view them as order takers. Because of that there is very little sales training taking place in the service department.

Again I want to remind you that it is not uncommon to average a 50% mark-up on parts and 75% on labor. These margins do not exist in the sales department! *So why aren't car dealers allocating more resources to service advisor training?*

Especially as the frequency of service visits is going down because of engineering improvements, synthetic oil, and over the air updates? We need better-trained service advisors now more than ever!

How much are you investing in your service advisor training? Are you tracking one line item repair orders? Are you properly staffed so your service advisors see no more than 12 customers per day? Are your advisors required to do an active walkaround and delivery?

If the answer is no to any of these questions then you are leaving lots of money on the table.

## 18.     Not selling parts online.

Again because majority of car dealers and general managers came up through sales they don't understand how profitable fixed ops could be.  Not selling parts online is only making it easier for independent parts stores.

***Store managers in NAPA and Pep Boys must be thanking their lucky stars that car dealers are completely asleep when it comes to selling parts online.***

If you really want to grasp e-commerce start with selling parts online.  The beauty of parts is that they are the same in all 50 states.  An oil filter in Oklahoma is the same as the oil filer in Oregon.  That means you are no longer limited by your local market.

In addition there are plenty of customers that are willing to pay for genuine OEM parts.  All you have to do is focus on marketing and e-commerce.

As I said before not many dealers have a dedicated advertising budget for parts and service.  Good news is that you can purchase a plug-in for your website with your OEM parts catalog.  Or you can start a separate website dedicated to selling OEM parts.

If you do it right you could be literally making money in your sleep.

## 19.     Not having service hours that are convenient to your customers.

Have you ever noticed that service department hours are different from sales hours?  I usually see service department hours to be 7-7 Monday to Friday, 8-5 on Saturdays, and closed on Sunday.

For some reason car dealers give people more opportunities to buy a car instead of servicing that car. Meanwhile margins on new car sales are evaporating while fixed ops margins are remaining strong.

In addition, customers have busy lives.  They have a job, sometimes more than one, they have kids that need to be taken to school or to a soccer practice, and they have spouses.  In other words people are busy living their lives and car dealers should accommodate their customers.  That's the only way to improve customer experience and increase service retention.

Inconvenient service hours mean one thing—your customers will go elsewhere.  Remember I told you that Jiffy Lube must be laughing all the way to the bank.  At the very minimum you need to stay open on Sundays. Better yet consider keeping your service department open until midnight.

Some progressive dealers I know stay open 24 hours and offer a vehicle pick-up at night and a vehicle return the next morning.  That's amazing service!

*I don't want to sound like a broken record but it is your service business that will carry you through the next economic downturn. Not to mention that happy service customers will buy more cars from your dealership.*

## 20.      Not selling vehicle service contracts in service drive.

Vehicle service contracts could be very profitable; just ask any finance manager.  Finance managers deserve a lot of respect because it is hard to sell a service contract on new or certified pre-owned car.

In my opinion it should be easier to sell vehicle service contracts in the service drive.  It's a much more natural habitat compared to the showroom.  *So why aren't service advisors selling service contracts like hot cakes?*

There are several factors at play.  First, there is no directive from the senior management team so basically it is not in their job description.  Second, they do not have the necessary training.  Finance managers that do this for a living have a hard time selling vehicle service contracts so it is imperative to provide regular training.  Third, service advisors do not have the time to pitch because they are overwhelmed.  I promise you that if your service advisors see more than 12 customers per day they will never be able to sell anything let alone a vehicle service contract.  Fourth, is the fact that most consumers cannot afford a vehicle service contract the same way they cannot afford a $1000 repair.  It is imperative to offer 0% APR financing in order to increase penetration.

The first step is for the dealer principal, general manager, or parts & service director to recognize this revenue stream and then provide training and the necessary support. It is also a good idea to set-up sales targets and bonuses for the advisors that hit the goal.

The main reason your customers are bombarded with phone calls and direct mail from third parties trying to sell them a vehicle service contract is because your dealership is not doing it.

*That's the funny thing about market economy—if you ignore needs of your customers someone will take care of them.*

## 21.    Not seeing the danger of OEM subscriptions.

Franchise laws prohibit car manufacturers to sell and lease vehicles directly to consumers.  Basically, it is the franchise law that keeps new car dealers in business.  It is also the franchise law that gives them a false sense of security.

Due to the franchise law carmakers really have no control over the sales process in the showroom.  I am convinced that carmakers feel that they can do a better job selling cars than dealers.  Here come OEM subscription models!  Subscription model completely eliminates car dealer from the equation.

You see the funny thing is that subscriptions are not sales or leases.  They are what attorneys call a grey area.  More importantly the concept of subscriptions didn't exist when franchise laws were written so technically speaking OEM's are not breaking the law.

At the time of this writing subscriptions represent a tiny percentage of new car sales but we are witnessing carmakers change consumers' behavior.  They are retraining consumers to go direct to the carmaker not the dealer to get a new car.  *That is alarming and dealers need to fight back before it is too late!*

Let's take Volvo for example.  Imagine you are a Volvo dealer.  Now you are not just competing with other Volvo dealers you are also competing with your own factory.  This is the same factory that is asking you to spend millions of dollars on facility upgrades.  This is the same factory that might hold your allocation because they want to use these cars for subscriptions.

Now let's take a look at what subscription model does to a Volvo dealer.  First, there is a lost sale.  Second, there is lost F&I revenue.  Third, there is lost fixed ops revenue.  All of that means reduction in dealership's workforce.

I am a member of Greater New York Automobile Dealer Association and they had a seminar dedicated to the franchise law.  Maybe 15 people showed up and majority of them were not dealer principals.  Dealer principals need to wake-up and see the danger of subscriptions.

*I want to urge car dealers to lobby their respective state dealer associations and put an end to this insanity!*

## 22.    Not understanding service and parts.

I spend my days visiting car dealers and more often than not I meet owners and general managers that do not understand fixed ops. In reality general manager is responsible for all departments but what I see is mostly general sales managers that are not involved and are not paid for the production in parts and service.

If you want all of your departments working towards the same the goal and be on the same page you need to have one person overseeing the entire operation. That is the only way!

Unfortunately there is no parts and service management major at a local university so it is important for dealer principals to provide training for general sales managers. Good place to start is NADA University. It is not cheap but totally worth it.

Less expensive solution is to move the dealer principal's or general manager's office to the service department. Being on the front line will keep service employees on their toes and will help you understand the business.

Mystery shopping is another great way to learn how your service department operates. If you call to make an appointment for an oil change and are told the next available appointment is Friday next week at 2pm you know you have a major issue. If you call to find the price of a break job and can't get someone on the phone or can't get a straight answer then you know you are losing this business to independent mechanics because they are much better at answering the phones.

*Understanding parts and service will help make more money, increase absorption, and improve customer experience.*

## 23.    Not mystery shopping.

Trust, but verify is a Russian proverb.  It became well known in the United States when used by President Ronald Reagan on many occasions in the context of nuclear disarmament.

As a dealer principal or a general managers you absolutely have to trust your team to do the right thing but you can't forget that path of least resistance is the default human behavior.  So how do you verify?  One of the most effective ways to keep your team on their toes is to mystery shop your dealership on a regular basis.  Your people must know that ANY customer at ANY given point could be a mystery shopper.  ***So why aren't car dealers doing this?***

My guess is that they are afraid to learn the truth.  Mystery shopping means rocking the boat.  And rocking the boat means reevaluating your processes, retraining your people and that means more work for you.  And nobody likes more work which brings me to my previous point—path of least resistance is the default human behavior.

If you want to stay competitive and improve customer experience then you absolutely must mystery shop all departments of your organization.  Do the following:
- Submit an online inquiry
- Make an incoming sales call
- Come to the showroom and buy a car (Yes buy a car!  Go through the entire process.)

- Go through F&I presentation
- Get insurance
- Take delivery of the car
- RDR the car (Yes RDR the car!  You can unwind it later.)
- Call service department to schedule an oil change
- Call service department to find a price of a break job or any other frequently requested repair
- Drive to the service department to see if service advisors are using an active walkaround
- Wait for the car to be repaired.  This way you will know if your techs are using a multi-point vehicle inspection and if your advisors are upselling

Repeat this process on a regular basis in order to fix broken systems.  I promise that you will be disappointed on many occasions in the beginning but as you work through the problems your organization will become stronger and more customer experienced focused.

## 24.    Wholesaling off-brand used cars.

Believe or not there are dealers that do that!  Talk about insanity!  Let's say you are a Lexus dealer.  It is not uncommon to take BMW, Acura, or Audi on trade. If the car is in good condition why would you wholesale it?  Get it front line ready and you will sell it.  Having variety of used cars will only increase your chances of retailing more cars.

Bad enough it is getting harder to make money selling new cars why would you limit your opportunities with used cars.  Last time I checked used cars is a huge profit center.

Putting all your eggs in one basket is a risky strategy and makes zero sense in the used car department.

## 25.    Not focusing on used car sales.

There are a lot of egomaniacs in car business.  They want to be number one at any cost and oftentimes this egomania is misguided.  Here is what I mean—for some crazy reason they want to be number one in NEW car sales.

When I was in retail I wanted to be number one in making money and in majority of cases profit margins are way better on used cars.  Think about it logically and you will see the beauty of used car sales.  Below are few reasons why you should focus on used car sales:

- No stair step
- Offer variety of makes and models to attract more buyers
- No CSI surveys
- Higher profit margins
- Greater vehicle service contract penetration
- Keep your service department busy (internal and customer pay labor)

### *Why aren't car dealers focusing more on used car sales?*

Because it requires more work!  Remember that whatever makes money is never easy.  You would need to get better at appraising, buying, and wholesaling cars.  You would need to understand importance of turning your inventory quickly.  You would need to retrain your sales staff.  You would need to change the way you advertise.  You would need to change pay plans.

So instead a lot of car dealers are obsessed with who can give away more new cars on any given month. Race to the bottom is not an effective strategy to make a living.

## 26.    Not displaying F&I products on the dealership website.

Let's do another experiment.  Got to any dealership website (start with your own) and most likely you will be able to do the following:

- Research different vehicles
- Find out a price of the vehicle
- Submit a credit application
- Make a service appointment
- Buy parts online (maybe)

One thing for sure – you won't be able to learn anything about F&I products being offered.  *F&I products are a dirty secret.*  Here is why: F&I department is one of the few remaining profit centers and the fear is that full disclosure will negatively impact product penetration and gross profit.

Because of Amazon and Uber we live in the age of complete transparency and consumers expect it when it comes to F&I products.  I want to urge car dealers to post all relevant information about F&I products they offer.  List all features and benefits, use charts and graphs in order to make the case why customers should buy various types of protection.  I strongly recommend listing the sales prices as well.  This is what transparency looks like.

Given the opportunity to do the research prior to coming to the dealership consumers are much more likely to say yes to F&I products. So what are you waiting for? Get your F&I products on the website ASAP!

## 27.     Not doing post-sale F&I product follow-up.

So here is what's going on in 99% of car dealerships. Customer gets into F&I, finance manager pitches some (not all) products, and if the customer says NO then nothing happens.  Customer is forgotten and the opportunity to pitch these products at a later point is wasted.

***The concept of post-sale F&I follow-up doesn't exist!*** I can't understand why but then again when I was in retail I didn't do it either.

Customers don't trust car dealers and they don't trust F&I managers.  In many cases customers come into F&I office with their guard up and say NO to all F&I products as a knee-jerk reaction because they read something online.

I am convinced that you will pick up additional F&I product sales if you follow-up with these customers in a week or two.  They will be at home or at work so they will no longer feel that they are in a threatening environment, they will have possession of the car and the pride of ownership.  It is totally worth it to pitch them products again.  What do you have to lose?

You need to decide whether your F&I or BDC department will do the actual follow-up.  My preference is on F&I because they have the necessary product knowledge and should be able to handle the sale from A to Z.

I would work with the BDC department to create a series of follow-up emails specifically dedicated to unsold F&I products. You could even include a link for the customers to do the online checkout and offer 0% APR financing as well.

***If you not going to do this I promise that someone else will.***

## 28. Using long term financing.

Cars are getting more expensive and interest rates are going up so there is an affordability issue. I get it. But offering long term financing such as 72, 84, or 96 months is not doing any good for your customers and for your business.

Long term finance means two things—your customers are guaranteed to be upside down and you are guaranteed not to sell them another car for a very long time. Both choices are pretty bad.

I know it is hard to close a customer on a higher payment so temptation to stretch out the term is always there. It is imperative that you train your desk managers and finance managers not to exceed 60 months terms under any circumstance. *This approach means additional training and culture change but your customers and your business will benefit from it.*

## 28.    Not using a menu in F&I.

A lot of dealers make a mistake and think that using a menu in F&I makes them compliant. News flash—there is no law on the books that requires you to use a menu. Unfortunately when you only use a menu as a "compliance tool" your finance managers will reject it or try to find a way to beat the system.

The only reason to use a menu is because it is an awesome sales tool. It allows you your dealership to enforce the 300% rule:

***Presenting 100% of your products to 100% of your customers 100% of the time.***

Finance managers are like the rest of us; they are creatures of habit. So if the finance manager is only comfortable pitching vehicle service contracts and GAP then these are the only two products that he or she will present.

Using a menu allows you to hold your finance department accountable and track product penetration. Tracking product penetration will help you make training and pay plan adjustments in order to increase it and make more money. For example, you can conduct a product knowledge training session to make sure that your finance managers are comfortable presenting all products. Another approach is to help them create powerful word tracks. In addition, you can offer an extra spiff if they sell a particular product.

It goes without saying that you should be using an electronic menu for the maximum effect. Your menu must push and pull data from your Dealer Management Software (DMS) to increase speed and accuracy. ***Unfortunately too many dealers are either not using a menu or using a handwritten paper menu.***

## 29.     Powerbooking used cars.

Just in case you don't know what I am talking about –
powerbooking means your finance department tells the
lender that a used car you are trying to sell comes with
leather, sunroof, navigation, alloy wheels, tow hitch,
roof racks, kitchen, and sink.  Finance managers do that
to get a greater advance from the bank so they can
maximize gross profit.

There are several reasons why this is a bad idea.  First,
you will most likely put the customer in a wrong car.  A
car that they cannot afford so the probability of them
going repo is much greater.  At that point I can say this
with a 100% certainty—*this customer is not coming
back to buy another car and you are not getting any
referrals.*

Second, you will be charged back by the lender for the
missing equipment. Now this lender will look at ALL of
your deals with a magnifying glass.  This will only make
it harder for you to get deals done so nobody needs to
strain their relationship with lenders.

Third, car business is a very small business where
everybody knows each other.  Bank reps change jobs as
often as finance managers do.  So your Ally Financial
rep today could be your Americredit rep tomorrow.
And guess what – he is not going to forget that your
finance managers powerbook used cars.

To avoid powerbooking you should two things. First, have a used car manager AND finance manager sign-off on the book-out sheet. Second, you must have a zero tolerance powerbooking policy in place. Zero tolerance means one strike and you are out.

Here is a final thought—banks no longer wait to repo the car to find out if it is missing equipment. They now conduct random equipment checks even if the customer is not past due. If there is a discrepancy they just send you a bill. Let that sink in...

## 30.     Not selling parts online.

This topic is very important so this is the second chapter dedicated to it. Independent parts stores are similar to independent mechanics—both must be laughing all the way to the bank because car dealers can't figure out how to do oil changes in a reasonable time without an appointment and how to sell parts online.

As I mentioned before it all starts with the fact that dealer principals and general managers do not understand fixed operations. Because of that there is hardly any innovation coming out of parts and service. Majority of dealerships don't have any substantial advertising budget dedicated to attracting customers to parts and service.

*No wonder NAPA, Pep Boys, and Jiffy Lube are thriving!* Selling parts online is the best way to learn e-commerce. There are several to do it. First, you can purchase an entire e-commerce solution that includes your OEM parts catalog, shopping cart, and shipping. You will then either plug it into your main website or build a dedicated website for parts sales.

Second, is to start selling parts on eBay. Some dealers are doing it and are pretty successful.

But let's be honest eBay is not what it used to be. The real eight hundred pound gorilla in the word of digital retail is Amazon. ***Why aren't you selling parts on Amazon?***

It is not easy but nothing worthwhile is. People trust Amazon, they trust Amazon Prime even more, and of course they trust a four star or higher rated seller. Your mission if you choose to accept it is to become an Amazon Prime seller with a high rating. One of my dealer clients has done just that and is averaging over 60% mark-up on this type of parts sales.

## 31.    Not being able to attract quality employees.

It is hard to find good people in any business and car business is no exception.  A lot of companies especially in information technology and investment banking understand that their long-term success depends on attracting talented people.  Companies such as Google, Facebook, Goldman Sachs, and Morgan Stanley are very active at college job fairs.  They offer summer internships and if the candidate fits their needs offer a full-time employment upon graduation.

These companies primarily are after Ivy League graduates and that's great news because there are literally thousands of colleges that are outside of Ivy League.  *When was the last time your dealership participated in college job fair?*  I am going to take a wild guess and say NEVER.

Now let's assume for a second that you are going to participate in the next college job fair in your town.  What do you have to offer?  Why college graduates should consider applying for a job at your dealership?  Are you going to win them over with bell-to-bell hours, all commission pay plan, no weekends, and absolutely no training?

No wonder there is total talent drought in car business.  It is so bad that you rarely see a high school graduate let alone a college grad.  Dealers have no problem employing people with criminal records, and are afraid to drug test job applicants.

***When you attract bottom of the barrel applicants you are guaranteed to get bottom of the barrel production.*** And that brings me to the next point: hiring useless managers.

## 32.     Hiring incompetent managers.

I am in dealerships almost every day and I am amazed at the low quality of senior managers that run these multi-million dollar businesses. A lot of these guys do not know the basics of business administration, organizational theory, and have zero understanding of automotive retail. Yet somehow they are gainfully employed. Here is how it works.

In most cases if you are looking for a job as a general manager someone has to refer you to the dealer principal. That means that whoever is referring you must think you know what you are doing. Then after interviewing several applicants dealer principal must think that you are the best available candidate. This is a real indication that even dealership owners do not understand their own business. They hand keys to the kingdom to people that do not read, can barely write, have no vision, and then act surprised why their business isn't growing.

It is hard to attract quality personnel but if you as a dealer principal have made a decision to hire a general manager or a service manager it is your responsibility to provide the necessary training. There are several ways to provide this training. ***The worse way is training on the job. It is the equivalent of blind leading the blind.*** Below are more effective ways to train:

- NADA University

- 20 Groups
- State Dealer Association
- Outside trainers
- NADA Show

Let's examine each training method in a greater detail. NADA University is expensive but worth every dollar. If you have children you absolutely must send them to NADA University to understand the theoretical framework of car business. If you hired a general manager you absolutely must to send him or her to NADA University to gain a big picture view of the business. 20 Groups are a great way to learn from other progressive dealers that are outside of your area. State dealer associations provide a comprehensive curriculum for managers, employees, and dealer principals. I am a member of Greater New York Automobile Dealer Association and attend their classes on a regular basis and unfortunately in most cases classrooms are half empty. Bringing outside trainers is a great way to learn a new way of doing business and to motivate your team. NADA Show takes place once a year in Las Vegas, San Francisco, or New Orleans. Vendors that service all departments exhibit there and you will see the latest innovations that you can implement in your dealership.

***Training is expensive and results are not immediate so instead some dealer principals would buy a Ferrari, or a plane, or a boat.***

Allocate $20 from each car sold and $2 from each Customer Pay repair order for sales, customer service, and leadership training and you will be light years ahead of your competition.

## 33.    Hiring General Sales Managers instead of General Managers.

Here is another paradox.  Most dealerships have a General Sales Manager and a Service Manager.  What they do not have is a General Manager.  ***How do you expect to steer the ship without a captain?***

Majority of GSM's and service managers do not see eye-to-eye.  That's why there is no coordinated marketing campaign, no proper sales to service hand-off, different business hours, higher internal repair orders, and the list goes on.

Every Fortune 500 company has a CEO who is responsible for the overall strategy and vision.  Dealerships are no different.  It is a mistake to think that the dealer principal is the CEO.  With a few exceptions dealer principals are either absent from the dealership (they have families, residences in several states, etc.) or they do not have the necessary knowledge themselves to run this very complex business.

***The most important job a dealer principal has is to find a competent leader and empower him or her to make sure that the dealership will grow and survive the cataclysmic shifts taking place in automotive retail.***

## 34.     Not offering home delivery.

Home delivery is a prominent part of today's shopping process.  People are busy with their lives, jobs, and families and if given a choice between going to the store or getting an item delivered a vast majority will opt for home delivery.  I don't remember last time I went to a pharmacy, Home Depot, and Best Buy.

It is no different when buying a car.  Why should I drive to the dealership instead of getting an office or home delivery?  Especially now that Carvana is offering a nationwide home delivery!  *So why aren't car dealers offering a home delivery?  Forget nationwide, not even in a twenty mile radius?*

The answer is simple – it means changing the way they do business and nobody likes change.  The problem is that if car dealers do not make the necessary changes and respond to the shift in consumers' shopping habits they risk complete extinction.  Just ask Blockbuster or Barnes & Nobel how ignoring these shifts worked out for them.

One of the main reasons for not delivering cars is F&I.  Dealer principals know that most likely they are not making any money selling a car so the hope for F&I to upsell a vehicle service contract and other ancillary products.  Home delivery endangers this approach but it doesn't have to.  Finance managers should use video conferencing tools such as Go To Meeting and present the menu to a customer who is not in the dealership. If there is a will there is a way.

Another reason is identity theft. All the red flags checks must be done prior to delivery and you should use notary services that are specialize in automotive home deliveries.

Final reason is logistics. You need to have staff available to do the home or office delivery. One of the easiest solutions is to send a driver in the customer's car and have him come back in an Uber.

*The best part is that customers are willing to pay for a home delivery. For example, Vroom a used car online retailer charges $499 for home delivery and they sold over 250,000 vehicles since their inception.*

So what are you waiting for? Home delivery will help you keep/gain customers and could be a nice profit center as well.

## 35.     Not selling cars online.

The longer you refuse to accept the fact that the world is changing the harder it is going to survive in the future.  By not addressing changes in consumers' shopping habits today car dealers are making it easier for Carvana, Vroom, and other disrupters gain market share.

Whether you like it or not but online car sales are here and they are here to stay.  For example, in the last six months Carvana sold 43,000 cars.  So it is up to you to make the changes in your sales process.

Online car sales are not going to eliminate traditional brick and mortar car buying.  The key is to give consumers multiple options when shopping for a car. Apple is a good example—you could shop online or in the Apple store.  Better yet you could go to the Apple store and learn about different products they offer and then go home and buy online.

You could start with a digital storefront from a Roadster and see what kind of response you are going to get from your customers.  The scary part for most car dealers is that online sales mean complete transparency and complete transparency means loss of gross profit.  Committing to online sales means switching to one price for cars and F&I products and that is change most car dealers are petrified of.  That's the reason car dealers continue to believe that customers like to haggle.  Talk about fake news...

## 36.    Not dealing with employee turnover.

There is a strong belief in car business that nobody is irreplaceable.  It is true to an extent but this is no way to run a business.  Employee turnover in car dealerships, especially in sales department is astronomical.  It exceeds 70%.

High turnover hurts customer experience and negatively impacts customer retention and profit margins.  It is also very expensive because you have to allocate resources to constantly hiring and training new staff.

***What does high turnover really mean?  It means your employees do not want to work for you.  Plain and simple.***  So the real question that every dealer principal and general manager needs to ask is WHY.

Let's address the most important factors that contribute to employee turnover:

- Schedule
- Pay plan
- Opportunity to grow
- Lack of training
- Organizational culture

Days of sales people being willing to work bell-to-bell hours and no days off during the last week of the month are long gone.  Millennials are cut from a different cloth and we need to recognize that.  As quality of life incrementally improves employees all over the world are willing to work less hours. Create a forty hour work week to attract sales people. The ones that are really motivated by money will work longer anyway.

All commission pay plans are no longer effective. Again millennials due to poor parenting are not motivated by money. Therefore it is virtually impossible to attract younger employees with a promise of no base salary and high commissions. Moreover, it is almost impossible to make money when you are a green pee. Base salary is very helpful, especially when sales people first start. You can always give them an option to take lesser salary and greater commission in the future once they learn the basics.

There must be an opportunity to grow and you should be able to articulate it. Sales people should have an opportunity to become sales managers or finance managers. Finance managers should have an opportunity to become finance directors or general managers. *General Managers should have an opportunity to become partners.* Mechanics should have an opportunity to become shop foremen, service advisors, or service managers. You get the idea. There should be well-defined criteria for promotion. Remember we live in the time of extremely low unemployment and nobody wants a dead-end job with no shot of advancing.

Lack of training sends a very simple message to employees that you do not care about them. Your employees will look for another job where training is provided. It is training that will help them become confident and have a clear path to advance their careers.

*CFO asks CEO: "What happens if we invest in developing our people and then they leave us?"*
*CEO: "What happens if we don't and they star?"*

Organizational culture is an important factor in attracting and retaining employees. It is the job of a dealer principal and senior management team to define and create organizational culture. Sell, sell, sell cannot be the cornerstone of your dealership culture. There are other factors to consider such as taking care of employees and customers and being active in the community.

If you refuse to recognize the simple fact that employee expectations today are different from the time you were in the tranches it will get progressively harder for your dealership to attract quality personnel and you will continue to suffer from high turnover.

## 37.      Not adding dealer-owned insurance brokerage business.

Some businesses complement each other.  For example, Nike is in business of selling sneakers and sports clothing.  Apple is in business of selling computers, phones, and tablets.

Selling car insurance is a logical extension for any car dealership with sales of 100 units per month.  That is 100 opportunities to offer automobile insurance.  There is also a tremendous opportunity in the service department.  Dealership that sells 100 cars a month most likely writes around 1500 repair orders.  That is another 1500 opportunities to provide a car insurance quote and switch customers to a less expensive premium. Not to mention the fact that you can cross-sell home, renters, and life insurance!  Your dealer-owned insurance brokerage will earn commissions and then renewals income as well.  *So why aren't more car dealers leaving so much money on the table?*

The answer is simple—again it requires a change in process, and that means more work, and there is no time to do any of that when you are chasing monthly stair-step or employ incompetent people that have no vision.

Allstate has a phenomenal program for car dealers or you can partner with a local broker.  Or you as a dealer principal can get a broker's license yourself.  There are many options but they all require massive action.

## 38. Not hiring professionals to work in the BDC department.

Business Development Center is becoming more critical every day. As consumers' shopping habits change they visit less dealerships before making a decision to buy. That means there is no margin for error when it comes to incoming internet leads or sales calls.

***So why are so many car dealers paying next to nothing to BDC reps and managers?*** We all know that you get what you pay for. Guess what you are going to get when you pay minimum wage or slightly more? Guess what kind of leader you are going to get to run your BDC department if you are paying $36,000 per year?

Let me save you some time and give you the answer—you are going to get complete incompetence to the 10$^{th}$ power. I hope you are recording your incoming sales calls and all you have to do is to listen to ANY call to see that I am right.

Automotive retail is changing in real time and we need to rethink the way we treat and compensate BDC employees. Maybe 15 or 20 years ago it was OK to pay very little but now we cannot afford to do that. There are incoming sales and service leads as well as outbound campaigns for sales and service retention. BDC is the real bloodline of your business. Do you think you will be able to find a competent sales manager for less than $120,000 per year? So why do you think that a $36,000 per year BDC manager is going to make the magic happen?  It is in your best interest to pay more in order to attract qualified personnel.  Stop thinking that you can promote a receptionist to be your BDC manager...

## 39.     Not reinsuring F&I products.

I provide income development services to dealers across the country and I can't tell how many are leaving money on the table by not reinsuring F&I products such as vehicle service contracts, paint and fabric protection, key replacement, etc.

Here is the simplified description of reinsurance.  In order to see the benefits of reinsurance you need to understand how insurance companies make money. They do it two ways:  first is through underwriting profit and second is investment income.  Underwriting profit is the premium dollars left over after all the claims are paid.   Insurance companies invest premium dollars in stocks and bonds and that's how they earn investment income.

Whenever you sell OEM products or third-party products you are only making money by marking them up.  There is nothing wrong with that approach but the income generated is considered ordinary income and taxed as such.

Instead you should set-up a reinsurance company and pay all the premiums to your reinsurance company. There are several jurisdictions that allow you to do that with zero start-up capital.  These jurisdictions are Turks & Caicos, Delaware Indian Tribe Territory, etc.

So what happens if claims exceed premium dollars in your reinsurance company?  Have no fear -- there is a real insurance company backing each vehicle service contract or ancillary product sold by your F&I department. In addition, there is an administrator that adjudicates claims and files taxes. There is a per contract admin fee that they charge but it is totally worth it.

Since you own the reinsurance company you will get to keep underwriting profits and investment income. The best part is that underwriting profit is not taxed and investment income is taxed as such not as ordinary income.

Furthermore, you are in complete control of claims. I strongly recommend using a mileage tieback. For example, if the customer's vehicle breaks down within a 30-mile radius they would have to do the repair at your service department. This way you ensure that your shop is loaded with work and the right work is being done. Another example, you can approve a claim that technically should be denied. You would do to make a really good customer happy. This type of flexibility is priceless.

The idea here is that you can build a real asset outside of your dealership and use the funds for business expansion or whatever else your heart desires.

Getting back to how hard it is to find good people. It is even harder to retain them. You could offer equity in your reinsurance company to your general manager or a finance director so they know that there is a light at the end of the tunnel.

CONTACT ME TO SET-UP A REINSURANCE PROGRAM AT YOUR DEALERSHIP:

917-903-0312
max@maxzanan.com

## 40.     Not offering dealership-branded F&I products.

Branding is important and brand extension is the easiest way to approach it.  There is a reason why Nissan or GM wants you to sell their branded F&I products.  They sold you are dream that customers trust their brand name and it would be so much easier to increase product penetration.

*These are the same companies that can barely build a car that consumers want to buy.  Pontiac Aztec is the best illustration of this point.*

So why not extend your own brand?!  After all customers are buying from you not the OEM.  In addition, your service retention will go through the roof.  Customers automatically assume that an ABC Ford vehicle service contract is only good at ABC Ford.  And you will make more money selling dealer-branded F&I products.

Here is proof—AutoNation the largest publicly traded auto group in the country attributes increase in F&I profit to selling AutoNation branded products.

## 41.     Not providing customer service training.

Do you really need to focus on customer service when you are the only game in town? Of course not! The problem is that you are not the only game in town. There are your direct competitors within a few miles of you. There is Carvana, Vroom, and Shift on the web, and there are leasing companies/brokers everywhere in New York and New Jersey.

***So why do car dealers act like customer service doesn't matter?*** A lot of car dealers missed the fact that online reviews matter. We live in the world where anything less than 4.9 is a total failure why do car dealers have a 3.5, 3.0 or even below 2.5 star rating. Do you honestly think that customers can't wait to come to your 2.5 star rated dealership?

Bad reviews are the outcome of bad customer service and it is customer service that needs to be addressed. Ask yourself a simple question: when was the last time you had an organization wide training session dedicated to customer service. Again I am going to save you time and effort—NEVER.

Customer service training means teaching your staff the necessary skills in order to increase customer satisfaction. Not to increase car sales or hours per repair order. You read it right—training dedicated to making customers happy.

Here is a sample review:

"They don't care about anything except taking your money. This place is by far the WORSE place to get a car. Their customer service is disgusting. All they car about is taking your money. The employees there are rude and nasty. Nobody there ever has answers to questions. I would tell every single person I know thinking about buying something from _____ to stay FAR away _____."

I omitted the name of the OEM and the car dealership to protect the guilty. By the way this review is over 6 months old. If you are business owner you should be all over these reviews. Customer review is a reflection of your staff, your processes, and your customer service.

If this review wouldn't prompt an emergency customer service training I don't know what will.

Customer service training should be part of onboarding of new hires and ongoing training of existing employees. Every single employee of a car dealership must be trained and retrained. From a receptionist all the way to the general manager.

Customer service training might be the most important investment you can make as a dealer principal. If your organization is guilty of providing bad customer service eventually there will be no customers whatsoever. Do not forget that customers have choices!

## 42.      Not taking advantage of Public Relations firms.

Breaking news—customers do not trust car dealers and federal regulators do not like car dealers. So there is an image issue that absolutely needs to be addressed.

In most cases car dealers are honorable business people that do the right thing and are involved and respected in their communities. Unfortunately there are a few bad apples that ruin it for everybody. In addition, every time there is a negative headline in the newspaper, TV, or internet it only reinforces negative views that consumers have and drives away these consumers from brick and mortar dealerships.

Fortunately automotive retail is not the only industry that has a bad reputation. There are many examples where effective crisis management and public relations strategy improves the image of the company or industry. Here is one of the best examples.

Johnson & Johnson, maker of Tylenol, experienced a catastrophic setback due to product tempering that caused deaths of seven people. Many companies wouldn't be able to recover from such a crisis; however, Johnson & Johnson employed a successful public relations strategy that not only minimized damage to the company's reputation but also led to sales rebounding to pre-crisis levels. This happened in the 80's and none of us think twice about buying Tylenol today.

National Automobile Dealer Association (NADA) should spearhead a national public relations campaign. There are close to 17,000 new car franchises in the country. If each rooftop contributes $100 per month that would pay for a 20 million a year public relations campaign. I guarantee that NADA will be able to hire the best PR firm on the planet and if the PR campaign is sustained over a period of 3 to 5 years there will be an overall image improvement.

Our industry desperately needs a makeover. There is an overabundance of negative information about car dealers in the press and online. Negative stereotypes that consumers have fuel the rise of Carvana and other disrupters. We need to offset the negative press with positive articles and videos that highlight all the good car dealers do in their communities. Our industry needs a charismatic spokes person. The longer we wait as an industry the harder it is going to get in the near future.

## 43.  Not emphasizing product knowledge in sales.

Car dealers could invest thousands of dollars in sales training but it would be pretty much pointless unless sales people have the necessary product knowledge. Product knowledge makes up for a lot of sales deficiencies.

Majority of car dealers rely on the OEM to provide product knowledge. OEMs do it via brochures and online classes. The problem here is that these online courses are not that exciting. Moreover, there are ways to beat the system—there is always one sales person who is really good at taking tests so oftentimes other sales people would pay him or buy him lunch if he takes all product knowledge tests for them. Funny thing is that everybody in the dealership knows that this cheating is going on. In reality this cheating is hurting the customer experience and sales/profits.

Here is a true story. I wanted to buy a Toyota 4Runner and the main feature that attracted me was ventilated seats. I went to Toyota.com and learned that only 4Runner Limited came with ventilated seats. Since I am in the business I reached out to three general managers of Toyota dealerships to find out if they had the car in stock and if it had ventilated seats. All three with absolutely certainty said that Limited didn't come with ventilated seats and that there was a mistake on Toyota's website. At that point I was so committed to buying it anyway that ventilated seats didn't matter anymore.  A few days later I went to pick up my new truck.  I got inside and guess what?  There was a knob that you turn to the right for heated seats and to the left for ventilated seats.

The moral of the story is that three Toyota dealerships had no product knowledge and spent plenty of energy convincing me that Toyota.com made a mistake instead of looking inside the car.  I still bought the car but many customers would've moved on to another brand and the sale would've been lost.

*I strongly recommend walkaround competitions. Assign each model to a different sales person and ask them to do a 5 minute walkaround during a Saturday morning meeting.*  Make sure that the winner gets a bonus, for example, $500.00.  Also, it is really helpful to record the best walkarounds and post them on your website and YouTube channel.

*Do not buy into the hype that customers come in knowing everything about the car.  Customers still have questions and your sales people need to be prepared.*

## 44. Not emphasizing product knowledge in F&I.

This topic is very important to me because I provide F&I products and training to car dealers across the country. *Unfortunately a lot of finance managers do not have the necessary product knowledge of the products they are selling.*

They have a general idea about the products but no real specifics. For example, they know that a vehicle service contract covers mechanical breakdowns but have a hard time explaining the difference between Gold and Platinum levels of coverage. Or they know that tire and wheel covers road hazard but not sure if cosmetic coverage is included, or if cosmetic coverage covers curb rash.

Like I mentioned before product knowledge offsets many sales deficiencies. In addition to mystery shopping dealer principals and general managers should ask their finance managers to pitch them products and ask questions to see if they have the necessary product knowledge.

*There is nothing wrong with having an F&I product knowledge competition. It is a good idea to video record the best VSC, tire and wheel, etc. presentation and post it on your website and YouTube channel.*

## 45.    Continue to engage in deceptive advertising.

One of the main reasons car dealers have a bad reputation is deceptive advertising. We all know what it is and I don't want to bore you with legal definition. Instead I will provide you with a much easier definition that anybody can understand.

In 1964 United States Supreme Court Justice was asked to define pornography in one of the cases. Justice Potter Stewart gave the best definition:

"I know it when I see it."

Same definition applies to deceptive advertising. It is your responsibility not to engage in deceptive advertising. Do not shift the blame on your advertising agency. It is imperative that your dealership doesn't do it because of several reasons. First, you will be caught and pay a huge fine. Remember there is a permanent record of all of your ads so Federal Trade Commission or your State Attorney General could go back in time for a retroactive penalty. Second, it really poisons the entire buying process for the consumer and reinforces their negative view of car dealers.

That $99 a month Toyota Camry is never $99; there is always a catch, always a surprise. Either the customer has to be a previous owner, have a modest $7500.00 down payment, or an 850 credit score. Once the customer learns that there is a catch the trust is broken and the negative view of car dealers is reinforced.

*Dealership deceptive advertising is one of the major factors behind the rise of Carvana. The more car dealers engage in deceptive advertising the more appealing Carvana's transparency becomes.*

# CONCLUSION

I am 42 years old and hitched my wagon to automotive retail. I've been in car business all my adult life and I absolutely love what I do. My biggest fear is that car dealers, by ignoring tectonic shifts in consumer buying habits, are digging their own graves. ***And that means that automotive retail my not survive the next 10 years.*** Not to sound selfish but the last thing I want to do is to start a new career at the tender age of 52. Consumers are so disappointed in brick and mortar dealerships that they are willing to give any start-up such as Vroom, Carvana, Shift, etc. a chance.

This is a zero sum game. The more cars are being sold by online disruptors the less cars are being sold by brick and mortar dealerships. Less cars sold will eventually mean less traditional car dealerships. And that means less jobs.

I am optimistic and believe that it is not too late to turn this situation around. My hope that this book is a wake-up call to dealer principals, general mangers, and dealership employees. ***If we as an industry do not adjust to the times, invest in training, compliance, customer service and stop leaving money on the table then we will be extinct.***

Amazon or Carvana will eat our lunch!

**CONTACT ME AND LET ME HELP YOU DEVELOP A GAME PLAN FOR YOUR DEALERSHIP TO FLOURISH IN THIS CHALLENGING ENVIRONMENT!**

**917-903-0312**
max@maxzanan.com

**THANK YOU FOR READING!!!**

# NOTES

# NOTES

# NOTES

# NOTES

# NOTES